Ripley Readers

All true and unbelievable!

Learning to read. Reading to learn!

LEVEL ONE Sounding It Out Preschool-Kindergarten
For kids who know their alphabet and are starting to sound out words.

learning sight words • beginning reading • sounding out words

LEVEL TWO Reading with Help Preschool-Grade 1
For kids who know sight words and are learning to sound out new words.

expanding vocabulary • building confidence • sounding out bigger words

LEVEL THREE Independent Reading Grades 1-3
For kids who are beginning to read on their own.

introducing paragraphs • challenging vocabulary • reading for comprehension

LEVEL FOUR Chapters Grades 2-4
For confident readers who enjoy a mixture of images and story.

reading for learning • more complex content • feeding curiosity

Ripley Readers Designed to help kids build their reading skills and confidence at any level, this program offers a variety of fun, entertaining, and unbelievable topics to interest even the most reluctant readers. With stories and information that will spark their curiosity, each book will motivate them to start and keep reading.

Vice President, Licensing & Publishing Amanda Joiner
Editorial Manager Carrie Bolin

Editor Jordie R. Orlando
Writer Korynn Wible-Freels
Designer Scott Swanson
Reprographics Bob Prohaska
Production Design Luis Fuentes

Published by Ripley Publishing 2020

10 9 8 7 6 5 4 3 2 1

Copyright © 2020 Ripley Publishing

ISBN: 978-1-60991-406-6

No part of this publication may be reproduced in whole or in part, stored in a retrieval system, or transmitted in any form by any means, electronic, mechanical, photocopying, recording, or otherwise, without written permission from the publisher.

For more information regarding permission, contact:
VP Licensing & Publishing
Ripley Entertainment Inc.
7576 Kingspointe Parkway, Suite 188
Orlando, Florida 32819

Email: publishing@ripleys.com
www.ripleys.com/books
Manufactured in China in May 2020.

First Printing

Library of Congress Control Number: 2020937128

PUBLISHER'S NOTE
While every effort has been made to verify the accuracy of the entries in this book, the Publisher cannot be held responsible for any errors contained in the work. They would be glad to receive any information from readers.

PHOTO CREDITS

Cover © salajean/Shutterstock **Master Graphics** Created by Scott Swanson **3** © salajean/Shutterstock **4-5** David Díez Barrio/Getty Images **6** Francesco Riccardo Iacomino/Getty Images **7** Westend61/Getty Images **8-9** krisanapong detraphiphat/Getty Images **10-11** Phuvich Chavitrutaigul/Getty Images **12-13** Jonathan Irish/Getty Images **14-15** Olivier Parent/Alamy Stock Photo **16** Mike Kemp/In Pictures via Getty Images **17** milehightraveler/Getty Images **18-19** Nathan L Roker/Getty Images **20-21** Pakin Songmor/Getty Images **22-23** © Vladimir Wrangel/Shutterstock **24-25** Nature Picture Library/Alamy Stock Photo **26-27** Matteo Colombo/Getty Images **28-29** CARSTEN PETER/SPELEORESEARCH & FILMS/National Geographic Image Collection **30-31** Henrik Sorensen/Getty Images

All other photos are from Ripley Entertainment Inc. Every attempt has been made to acknowledge correctly and contact copyright holders and we apologize in advance for any unintentional errors or omissions, which will be corrected in future editions.

LEXILE®, LEXILE FRAMEWORK® , LEXILE ANALYZER®, the LEXILE® logo and POWERV® are trademarks of MetaMetrics, Inc., and are registered in the United States and abroad. The trademarks and names of other companies and products mentioned herein are the property of their respective owners. Copyright © 2020 MetaMetrics, Inc. All rights reserved.

Ripley Readers

Caves!

All true and unbelievable!

a Jim Pattison Company

Hello in there! This cave is dark and deep!

A cave is a hole in a hill or under the ground.

Caves are all over the world, from mountain tops to under the water.

You can find them where it is hot, cold, sunny, or snowy.

Water, wind, and moving rocks break down stone to make caves.

Lava and ice can make them, too!

Caves are very old and take many years to form.

Some caves were around with the dinosaurs!

A cave is like a maze in the earth!

This one goes on for miles. Do you think you could find the end?

When mineral water drips from the top of a cave, it makes a stalactite.

They come in a lot of shapes. These are called soda straws!

When minerals pile up on the ground, they make a stalagmite.

They can be big or small. Some of them are taller than you!

Why can't your eyes
see in a cave?

There is no light! It is
too dark!

Some caves are so deep that a skyscraper could fit in them!

Want to know something cool?

Blind cavefish do not have eyes! Caves are so dark they don't need them!

Did you know that bats are not really blind?

This cave is home to twenty million of them!

Blue and green glow worms can light up a cave!

Just look at how pretty they are!

Some of the white crystals in this cave are as long as a school bus!

Going into a cave is called spelunking.

Do you want to explore a cave someday?

Ripley Readers

All true and unbelievable!

Ready for More?

Ripley Readers feature unbelievable but true facts and stories!

For more information about Ripley's Believe It or Not!, go to www.ripleys.com